Journey through the Song of Solomon

a devotional

This Journal belongs to:

name

phone

date

uniquedove
creations

Kansas City, Missouri
www.uniquedove.com

by
chérie
blair

Journey through the Song of Solomon

by Chérie Blair
Text is revised from Mike Bickle's teachings on
the Song of Solomon. Used by permission.
Forward by Mike Bickle. Preface by Lisa Gottshall.
Closing Word by Audra D. Close.

Photography, artwork, typesetting, cover design, layout, and
editing by Chérie Blair. Edited by Audra D. Close, Debby Close,
and Lisa Gottshall. Capitalization has been added for emphasis.

Printed in the United States of America

ISBN 978-0-615-17374-0

If you find my beloved...

tell him I am lovesick!

Song 5:8 NKJV

This book is dedicated to
Jesus Christ!

My *Beloved* is
better than any love on earth! His leadership
is *perfect.* My Husband is
handsome; He is truly *dazzling!*
He is altogether lovely. He is
my best *friend!*

Song 5:10-11, 16 CBPV

Foreword

by Mike Bickle

It is my privilege to recommend this prayer journal as a tool to help you journey into intimacy and mature partnership with Jesus Christ. Chérie Blair has been on staff and served in various aspects of ministry with us at the International House of Prayer since January, 2003. She has heeded my encouragement to make the Song of Solomon a lifelong pursuit by turning it into devotional prayer. I believe a fragrance will arise from many who meditate on this Divine Love Song. These expressions will serve to empower and purify the Church before the Lord's return.

In 1988, the Lord spoke to me by His audible voice while praying, "Let Jesus seal my heart with the seal of His love" (Song 8:6). The Lord said that He would release grace to walk in Song 8:6-7 across the Body of Christ worldwide. He also made clear that this should be a primary focus for my ministry. After reading the Song of Solomon, I was perplexed. At first, I was intimidated by the terminology but soon found delight as I encountered our Bridegroom Jesus in the Song. I believe the Bride of Christ is the entire Church filled with mature love. Theologically, all believers are betrothed to Jesus (2 Cor. 11:2). The consummation of the marriage with the Lamb occurs in the age to come (Rev. 19:7). Our maturity is ultimately the fruit of Jesus' work on the Cross, His intercession, and the revelation of His glory and ravished heart for us. I pray the Lord will draw you after Himself in intimacy that you may run together with Him in ministry as you grow in greater passion for Jesus!

Mike Bickle, Director
International House of Prayer of Kansas City

...The Lord is our God, the Lord alone.

You shall *love* the Lord

your *God* with all your heart,

and with all your soul, and with all your might.

Keep these words

that I am commanding you today

in your heart.

Recite them

to your children

and *talk about them*

when you are at home and when you are away,

when you lie down and when you rise.

Bind them as a sign on your hand,

fix them as an emblem on your forehead,

and *write them* on the

doorposts of your house and on your gates.

Deuteronomy 6:4-9 NRSV

Preface

by Lisa Gottshall

God's Word is alive and able to change us on the inside. One of the most powerful ways to experience God's heart in His Word is by praying it back to Him. When we engage our hearts in dialogue with God Himself over His Word it becomes more than information. It becomes part of who we are — how we think, feel, and speak. The Holy Spirit yearns jealously within us. He loves to make God known to our hearts. He waits for us to come to Him in heartfelt conversation concerning the truths He has given. For example, what do we do with Jesus' unfathomable words, "As the Father has loved Me, so have I loved you" (John 15:9 NIV)? Do we believe this? As we confess God's Word our minds are renewed. We begin to move from doubt to faith and say, "Jesus, just as the Father has never wavered at all in His delight over You, so Your joyful love over me has never diminished in the least. You love me the same way, effortlessly and constantly." When I pray His words back to Him my inmost thoughts are confronted with the truth. Hindrances of fear and unbelief are exposed. Freedom comes when we experience God's truth deep within (John 8:32).

Chérie and I have spent many hours together discussing, praying, and singing the words of the Song of Solomon. Through her journey of communing with God in His Word, Chérie has been equipped with tools to help others deepen their walk with the Lord. I am grateful for this book. Experiencing the exchange between God's heart and mine over His Word is the most exhilarating pleasure I have ever known and is available to every believer. I pray this journal would be a tool that empowers you to cultivate a place of encounter with Christ in His Word so you may taste of His goodness over and over again. Be encouraged on your journey; it takes time to sow seeds that spring up into a garden.

Lisa Gottshall, Staff
International House of Prayer of Kansas City

Thy *Word* have I hid in mine *heart...*

Psalm 119:11

Introduction

to the Song of Solomon

This introduction is intended only to paint the initial brush strokes on a blank canvas that will become a glorious masterpiece as you journey with the Lord through the Song of all Songs.

The Song of Solomon is a Divine poetic Love Song inspired by the Holy Spirit to magnificently express the truth of Scripture and illustrate the Gospel of Christ. It is often translated as an allegory between Jesus Christ and His Bride — individual believers or the corporate Church.

There are three primary characters. King Solomon, depicted as the Bridegroom, represents the triumphant resurrected Jesus Christ who is Lord of lords and King of kings. The Shulamite woman is a picture of the Bride of Christ who will eventually experience full spiritual maturity. The Daughters of Jerusalem represent the spiritual condition of dullness and immaturity characteristic of many believers.

The ultimate goal of studying this Song is to cultivate a lifestyle of whole-hearted love and pursuit of our Beloved Bridegroom, Jesus Christ. I first discovered the Lord as my Eternal Bridegroom when someone encouraged me to read the Song of Solomon as a love letter from Jesus. I had been looking to earthly loves until 'I found the One my heart loves. I held him and would not let him go' (Song 3:4 NIV). I began to journal the Song in the form of prayers to Jesus and His responses to me. My heart soared with new passion for my Beloved. The Lord continually uses this Song to establish me in my identity as His Bride and to awaken my heart with greater love for Him.

We can each identify with the Shulamite's journey, which parallels various seasons through our own life experiences. May the Lord encounter your heart as you journey through the Song of Solomon by turning it into devotional prayer.

My soul *thirsts* for God,
for the *living God...*

Psalm 42:2 NKJV

8 *Revelations*

of Jesus Christ

The Song of Solomon reveals eight facets of Jesus' personality.
Each reflects a unique aspect of His relationship with the Bride.

1   Song 1:8   The Counseling Shepherd
                                       serves the Bride

2   Song 1:12-2:6   The Affectionate Father
                                       grants assurance of enjoyment

3   Song 2:8-9   The Sovereign King
                                       has authority over all things

4   Song 3:6-8   The Safe Savior
                                       brings peace and security

5   Song 4:1-15   The Heavenly Bridegroom
                                       expresses Bridal affection

6   Song 5:2   The Suffering Servant
                                       calls the Bride to join Him

7   Song 5:10-16   The Majestic God
                                       reveals His splendor

8   Song 8:6-7   The Consuming Fire
                                       displays supernatural love

7 Longings
of the human heart

1 We long *to be fascinated.* In the heart of every human being is a desire to marvel and experience wonder. Usually, we attempt to satisfy this need with secular entertainment, which leaves us craving still more. This longing is only fulfilled through the revelation of Jesus Christ, our beautiful Bridegroom King, as we experience the superior pleasure of knowing the depths and mysteries of God (1 Cor. 2:9-10; 4:1).

2 We long *to feel beautiful.* Our culture directs us to answer this desire with vanity. God has instructed us to focus not merely on our physical appearance but on the 'incorruptible beauty of a gentle and quiet spirit' (1 Peter 3:3-5 NKJV). He fulfills this longing by imparting revelation of Divine beauty to our hearts.

3 We long *to be great.* Whether we admit it or not, everyone deeply desires to experience nobility and honor. This longing is satisfied when we understand the truth that we will one day be enthroned and reign at the right hand of Jesus (Rev. 3:21).

4 We long *for intimacy without shame.* Knowing God fully as we are known by Him is true intimacy (1 Cor. 13:12). The mystery Paul speaks of is one of a marriage partnership between Jesus Christ and the Church (Eph. 5:31-32). The One who created us — our Maker, the God of the whole earth, the Lord of Hosts — is our Husband (Is. 54:5). We will be One with Jesus as He and the Father are One (John 17:20-26). The fullness of intimacy for which we yearn can only be entered into through the revelation of our eternal Bridegroom's affections.

5 We long *to be enjoyed.* Driven by a spirit of rejection we look to a multitude of counterfeits seeking acceptance. God not only accepts us; He likes us! He loved us so much that He gave us His only Son, Jesus Christ, who died and rose on our behalf (John 3:16; 2 Cor. 5:15). When we are lost He eagerly pursues us, and all of heaven rejoices when one sinner repents (Luke 15). The Lord delights in us (Is. 62:4). His desire is for us (Song 7:10). We are sought after, forgiven, and enjoyed by God. The sum of God's thoughts toward us are infinite (Ps. 139:17). The revelation of Jesus' finished work on the Cross and God's thoughts toward us satisfies our desire to be enjoyed. His everlasting love causes our hearts to overflow with springs of Living Water (John 4:14; 7:38).

6 We long *to be wholehearted.* We want to know the joy of lovesickness and the exhilaration of wholehearted love. Jesus speaks tenderly in the wilderness causing us to return to our true Husband (Hos. 2:7, 14, 16). He uses our cravings and wounds of broken love to lead us into the Heavenly Romance. As Divine love is imparted to our hearts wholehearted love for Jesus becomes our primary passion in life.

7 We long *to make a lasting impact.* We enjoy making significant contributions that change lives. Jesus invites His Bride to partnership. Together with the Lord we will fulfill His mandate to disciple all nations. As we draw near to God He imparts anointing for service. Every act of love during our internship on the earth will reap an eternal reward (Matt. 10:42; Rev. 22:12).

God created each of us with these desires. We cannot repent of the 'longings' He placed in our hearts. Instead we must turn from pursuing 'other lovers' (Hos. 2:7) and return to our First Love as we recognize that only God can satisfy us.

The unfolding of

your words

gives *light...*

Psalm 119:130 NIV

Instructions

for each devotional

Please use this devotional to study, pray, and journal through the Song of Solomon. You may journal the entire Song first and return later for more in-depth research. This study tool simply provides an on-ramp to praying the Scriptures as you journey through the Romance of the Gospel. If it becomes another assignment on your checklist set it aside. Ask the Lord to give you hunger for His Word. The goal is not that we understand all mysteries and knowledge without love (1 Cor. 13:2). It is about 'heart-movements' toward the Lord. As we draw near to God He draws near to us (James 4:8). We abide daily in God's Word so that we may bear fruit and fulfill the Greatest Commandments of loving the Lord, our God, with our entire beings and loving others as ourselves (Mark 12:30-31; John 15:4-8).

Some descriptive phrases serve as metaphors for intimacy with God. The phrase 'kisses of His mouth' communicates the revelation of God's Word to our hearts. We are NOT to think of kissing Jesus on the mouth. This is entirely outside the boundaries of God's Word. We renounce all interpretations of the 'kisses of the Word' that come from sensual imagination. Ask the Holy Spirit for revelation on imagery in the Song.

1. Read it

    a. First, read the whole book of the Song of Solomon three times. You may also read Ecclesiastes as a precursor to glean from the Song in the context of its progression from meaningless pursuits of life under the sun to the highest pursuit of Love.

    b. Read each new chapter several times before journaling it.

    c. Read the Scripture you are studying in three Bible translations: your own Bible, a second translation of your choice, and in the King James Version provided throughout this devotional.

2. Write it

a. Copy the verse directly from your Bible on the lines provided.

b. Create your Personal Paraphrase Version (PPV). Abbreviate your PPV by using your initials. For instance, John Smith would call his paraphrased version the JSPV. Summarize each phrase of a Scripture in your own words. Example: "The most excellent Love Song ever written, which expresses the heart of a Bridegroom King" (Song 1:1 JSPV).

c. Begin researching the passage to learn its context, meaning, and significance. Start by recording key words, questions, and insights. Look up cross-references and record your findings. You can write down your initial observations in this journal. Of course, you will need another blank notebook for more extensive study.

   After completing this devotional you may decide to return to specific verses for further study. Always use Scripture as your primary source to determine the Biblical interpretation of key words or phrases. You may gain additional insight through Bible dictionaries, concordances, lexicons, encyclopedias, and online resources. Reserve commentaries, books, and teachings to use once you have spent time researching and drawing your own conclusions. You will not answer every question immediately. This is a lifelong journey into the heart of Jesus Christ.

d. Create a Cross-Reference Version (CRV) by combining verses. Cut and paste portions of Scripture into your CRV to translate the Song of Solomon using Bible quotes. Include entire sentences or insert short phrases. Select verses from a context that would accurately portray the meaning of Scripture being translated. Try not to paraphrase the cross-reference except for pronouns. Please note: Each Bible translation has copyright guidelines. The King James Version, in public domain, can be used freely.

Example of a CRV for Song 1:2:

"...may God give [me] Of the dew of heaven..." (Gen. 27:28 NKJV), "...the spirit of wisdom and revelation..." (Eph. 1:17 NKJV), "...like a kiss on the lips" (Prov. 24:26 NIV). "...You have the words of eternal life" (John 6:68 NKJV). "Satisfy [me] with your unfailing love..." (Ps. 90:14 NLT), "For great is your love, higher than the heavens..." (Ps. 108:4 NIV). "How priceless is your unfailing love..." (Ps. 36:7 NIV); "...I desire you more than anything on earth" (Ps. 73:25 NLT). "You satisfy me more than the richest feast..." (Ps. 63:5 NLT) — "...Your love is better than life..." (Ps. 63:3 NIV).

3. Say it

Speak or sing the verse aloud. Say the verse throughout the day and commit it to memory. Form a Bible study discussion group.

4. Pray it

Turn your studies into prayerful expressions. Thank God for a particular truth He revealed to you through a passage. Ask Him for greater revelation and help to believe it. For example, "Lord, thank you that I am beautiful. Help me to see myself as You see me and to believe that I have both inner and outer beauty." Commit your heart to obey God's words of instruction. You could pray, "God, I will humble myself and repent whenever you show me hidden areas of sin and compromise, which keep me from bearing eternal fruit for Your Kingdom."

Continue meditating on a set of verses and praying from them while going about your day. Isolate a phrase and develop it by singing spontaneously from your heart. Interpret the passage through dance, art, or various forms of creativity. Use the blank pages to worship God through creative expression.

Open thou mine *eyes*, that I may behold *wondrous* things . . .

Psalm 119:18

Highlights
for Scripture meditation

Read it

Choose one version of the Bible to read from consistently
and one or more translations to read for comparison.
When meditating on a particular passage, start by reading
the entire chapter or book three times. After learning the
context, begin to focus on only a few verses at a time.

Write it

Keep a blank journal or notebook with your Bible to record
Scriptures, observations, questions, thoughts, and prayers.
Copy a few verses directly from your Bible to your journal.
Write the verse a second time in your own words adding
insights and other Scriptural references to look up later.
Create paraphrase and cross-reference versions.

Say it

Speak the Scriptures aloud and then turn them into songs
as you spontaneously sing through a passage. Join others
in small groups to discuss what God is teaching you.

Pray it

Pray each Scripture to the Lord thanking Him for a
particular truth and committing your heart to follow His
instruction in obedience. Also, pray through each
passage as a response from Jesus. Highlight truths from
His Word that He would say to encourage your heart.
You may enjoy turning your prayer into creative expressions
through music, dance, and various forms of visual art.

Listen to me,

O royal *daughter;*

take heart what I say.

Forget your people and your family far away.

For your royal *husband*

delights in your beauty;

honor him, for he is your *lord.*

Psalm 45:10-11 NLT

Song of Solomon 1

¹ The song of songs, which is Solomon's. ² Let him kiss me with the kisses of his mouth: for thy love is better than wine. ³ Because of the savour of thy good ointments thy name is as ointment poured forth, therefore do the virgins love thee. ⁴ Draw me, we will run after thee: the king hath brought me into his chambers: we will be glad and rejoice in thee, we will remember thy love more than wine: the upright love thee. ⁵ I am black, but comely, O ye daughters of Jerusalem, as the tents of Kedar, as the curtains of Solomon. ⁶ Look not upon me, because I am black, because the sun hath looked upon me: my mother's children were angry with me; they made me the keeper of the vineyards; but mine own vineyard have I not kept. ⁷ Tell me, O thou whom my soul loveth, where thou feedest, where thou makest thy flock to rest at noon: for why should I be as one that turneth aside by the flocks of thy companions? ⁸ If thou know not, O thou fairest among women, go thy way forth by the footsteps of the flock, and feed thy kids beside the shepherds' tents. ⁹ I have compared thee, O my love, to a company of horses in Pharaoh's chariots. ¹⁰ Thy cheeks are comely with rows of jewels, thy neck with chains of gold. ¹¹ We will make thee borders of gold with studs of silver. ¹² While the king sitteth at his table, my spikenard sendeth forth the smell thereof. ¹³ A bundle of myrrh is my well-beloved unto me; he shall lie all night betwixt my breasts. ¹⁴ My beloved is unto me as a cluster of camphire in the vineyards of Engedi. ¹⁵ Behold, thou art fair, my love; behold, thou art fair; thou hast doves' eyes. ¹⁶ Behold, thou art fair, my beloved, yea, pleasant: also our bed is green. ¹⁷ The beams of our house are cedar, and our rafters of fir.

Chapter One Overview

If we surrender our lives to Jesus Christ, our Savior, we are His eternal Bride. Our journey into mature partnership with our Bridegroom begins with longing for the kisses of God's Word. The Lord imparts His Word to our hearts causing us to cry for deeper intimacy with Him. We soon discover that God's affection is more satisfying than all earthly pleasures. This revelation awakens fervency to love the Lord with all our hearts, souls, minds, and strength as He leads us into the place of abiding in the Vine through intimate communion with Jesus.

At the onset of our journey, we are marked with the 'paradox' of grace. We see the reality of our sinful desires yet realize we are lovely in the eyes of God. Jesus, the **Counseling Shepherd**, compassionately teaches us the way forward in our weakness. We ask, "Where will You feed me?" He says, "Most beautiful, stay connected with other believers. Take care of the little ones I give you. Keep a right spirit towards imperfect leaders." He then declares, "My love, you are like a trained horse in righteousness, though you are young. The very hand of God Himself has touched your emotions. Your will (neck) is under the authority of God, the King. You will be Christ-like in character and used to deliver others."

Jesus expresses the heart of the **Affectionate Father** by embracing and affirming us at His table of redemption. Here we receive increasing revelation of the Salvation Jesus provided for us through the Cross. We understand the abundance of His suffering for love. In response, our fragrant worship ascends to God as perfume. As Jesus emphasizes our beauty and singleness of vision we recognize both Jesus' beauty and our spiritual pleasure in Him. His loveliness penetrates our spirits. We rest in Jesus — our eternal house of intimacy, fragrance, and security.

In this season of our journey we may think of the Lord primarily in terms of what we receive from God instead of what the Lord receives from us. We feel the pleasure of His nearness. Obedience to Jesus is not yet our highest goal in life; however, the Lord strategically leads us to slow down, receive His love, and eventually carry His love to others.

Song 1:1-3

¹ The song of songs, which is Solomon's.
² Let him kiss me with the kisses of his mouth:
for thy love is better than wine.
³ Because of the savour of
thy good ointments
thy name is as ointment
poured forth, therefore do
the virgins love thee.

date

1. Read it

2. Write it

Alternate Bible Version

Personal Paraphrase Version (PPV)

Key Words

Questions

Insights

Cross-Reference Version (CRV)

3. Say it

4. Pray it

1:1-3

Prayer to Jesus

Thanksgiving

Commitment

Jesus' Response

Creative Worship

Song 1:4

Draw me, we will run after thee: the king hath brought me into his chambers: we will be glad and rejoice in thee, we will remember thy love more than wine: the upright love thee.

date

1. Read it

2. Write it

Alternate Bible Version

___

___

___

___

___

Personal Paraphrase Version (PPV)

___

___

___

___

___

___

___

Key Words

Questions

Insights

Cross-Reference Version (CRV)

3. Say it

4. Pray it

1:4

Prayer to Jesus

Thanksgiving

Commitment

Jesus' Response

Creative Worship

Song 1:5-6

⁵ I am black, but comely, O ye daughters of Jerusalem, as the tents of Kedar, as the curtains of Solomon. ⁶ Look not upon me, because I am black, because the sun hath looked upon me: my mother's children were angry with me; they made me the keeper of the vineyards; but mine own vineyard have I not kept.

date

1. Read it

2. Write it

Alternate Bible Version

Personal Paraphrase Version (PPV)

Key Words

Questions

Insights

Cross-Reference Version (CRV)

3. Say it

4. Pray it

1:5-6

Prayer to Jesus

Thanksgiving

Commitment

Jesus' Response

Creative Worship

Song 1:7

date

1. Read it

2. Write it

⁷ Tell me, O thou whom my soul loveth, where thou feedest, where thou makest thy flock to rest at noon: for why should I be as one that turneth aside by the flocks of thy companions?

Alternate Bible Version

Personal Paraphrase Version

Key Words

Questions

Insights

Cross-Reference Version (CRV)

3. Say it

4. Pray it

1:7

Prayer to Jesus

Thanksgiving

Commitment

Jesus' Response

Creative Worship

Song 1:8

date

1. Read it

2. Write it

8 If thou know not, O thou
fairest among women,
go thy way forth by
the footsteps of the flock,
and feed thy kids beside
the shepherds' tents.

Alternate Bible Version

Personal Paraphrase Version (ppv)

Key Words

Questions

Insights

Cross-Reference Version (CRV)

3. Say it

4. Pray it

1:8

Prayer to Jesus

Thanksgiving

Commitment

Jesus' Response

Creative Worship

Song 1:9-11

date

1. Read it

⁹ I have compared thee, O my love, to a company of horses in Pharaoh's chariots. ¹⁰ Thy cheeks are comely with rows of jewels, thy neck with chains of gold. ¹¹ We will make thee borders of gold with studs of silver.

2. Write it

Alternate Bible Version

Personal Paraphrase Version (ppv)

Key Words

Questions

Insights

Cross-Reference Version (KJV)

3. Say it

4. Pray it

1:9-11

Prayer to Jesus

Thanksgiving

Commitment

Jesus' Response

Creative Worship

Song 1:12-14

¹² While the king sitteth at his table,
my spikenard sendeth forth the smell thereof.
¹³ A bundle of myrrh is my well-beloved unto me;
he shall lie all night betwixt my breasts.
¹⁴ My beloved is unto me as a
cluster of camphire in
the vineyards of Engedi.

date

1. Read it

2. Write it

Alternate Bible Version

Personal Paraphrase Version (PPV)

Key Words

Questions

Insights

Cross-Reference Version (CRV)

3. Say it

4. Pray it

1:12-14

Prayer to Jesus

Thanksgiving

Commitment

Jesus' Response

Creative Worship

Song 1:15-17

¹⁵ Behold, thou art fair, my love; behold, thou art fair; thou hast doves' eyes. ¹⁶ Behold, thou art fair, my beloved, yea, pleasant: also our bed is green. ¹⁷ The beams of our house are cedar, and our rafters of fir.

date _____

1. Read it

2. Write it

Alternate Bible Version

_____

_____

_____

_____

_____

Personal Paraphrase Version (PPV)

_____

_____

_____

_____

_____

_____

_____

Key Words

Questions

Insights

Cross-Reference Version (KJV)

3. Say it

4. Pray it

1:15-17

Prayer to Jesus

Thanksgiving

Commitment

Jesus' Response

Creative Worship

Song of Solomon | 2

¹ I am the rose of Sharon, and the lily of the valleys. ² As the lily among thorns, so is my love among the daughters. ³ As the apple tree among the trees of the wood, so is my beloved among the sons. I sat down under his shadow with great delight, and his fruit was sweet to my taste. ⁴ He brought me to the banqueting house, and his banner over me was love. ⁵ Stay me with flagons, comfort me with apples: for I am sick of love. ⁶ His left hand is under my head, and his right hand doth embrace me. ⁷ I charge you, O ye daughters of Jerusalem, by the roes, and by the hinds of the field, that ye stir not up, nor awake my love, till he please. ⁸ The voice of my beloved! behold, he cometh leaping upon the mountains, skipping upon the hills. ⁹ My beloved is like a roe or a young hart: behold, he standeth behind our wall, he looketh forth at the windows, shewing himself through the lattice. ¹⁰ My beloved spake, and said unto me, Rise up, my love, my fair one, and come away. ¹¹ For, lo, the winter is past, the rain is over and gone; ¹² The flowers appear on the earth; the time of the singing of birds is come, and the voice of the turtle is heard in our land; ¹³ The fig tree putteth forth her green figs, and the vines with the tender grape give a good smell. Arise, my love, my fair one, and come away. ¹⁴ O my dove, that art in the clefts of the rock, in the secret places of the stairs, let me see thy countenance, let me hear thy voice; for sweet is thy voice, and thy countenance is comely. ¹⁵ Take us the foxes, the little foxes, that spoil the vines: for our vines have tender grapes. ¹⁶ My beloved is mine, and I am his: he feedeth among the lilies. ¹⁷ Until the day break, and the shadows flee away, turn, my beloved, and be thou like a roe or a young hart upon the mountains of Bether.

Chapter Two Overview

Although we are immature in love the Lord affirms our beauty, which prepares us to grasp another dimension of our identity in Jesus. Some commentaries say Jesus is the rose while many others say the Bride is the rose. Both are true. With revelation of the redemptive riches in Christ we discover our highest identity as His Bride. We are the fragrance of Christ amidst this fallen world.

Confidence in our Bridal identity is essential to experiencing Jesus as the One who provides spiritual refreshment. When we experience God's enjoyment of us we enjoy God. We will never enjoy the Lord more than we comprehend His love for us when we are weak (Rom. 5:6-8; 1 John 4:10). At the Cross (shade tree) He provides nourishment that leads to joy in His presence. We no longer live under the shame of condemnation. His banner of Love now defines our lives. He causes negative circumstances to work for our good (Rom. 8:28).

Such spiritual pleasure awakens desire in us for deeper experiences of intimacy with Jesus. We begin to pray, "Give me more of God!" It is through the ministry of the Holy Spirit that we receive the fullness of God's love. The Lord strategically uses Divine seasons of personal satisfaction to cultivate spiritual growth while solemnly charging those believers who lack spiritual discernment not to rush the process of love. He cautions others to be gentle with His fervent yet easily distracted Bride. The Lord leads us into the next season when He knows it is best.

When the voice of God calls us we are confronted with a second spiritual crisis: fear. Jesus knocks on the door of our hearts challenging us to leave our comfort zones and inviting us to join Him in partnership. We ask, "Is Jesus Christ a safe God? Is it safe to obey Him completely?" He is calling us to face our fears. When tempted to refuse His invitation He tells us to keep lifting our voices to Him. He wants us to run to Him in our shame, not from Him. Convicted by the Holy Spirit we cry to God for deliverance from compromise. Jesus responds as the **Sovereign King** who effortlessly conquers all opposition.

Song 2:1-2

¹⁵ I am the rose of Sharon, and
the lily of the valleys.
² As the lily among thorns,
so is my love among
the daughters.

date

1. Read it

2. Write it

Alternate Bible Version

_____

_____

_____

_____

_____

Personal Paraphrase Version (PPV)

_____

_____

_____

_____

_____

_____

Key Words

Questions

Insights

Cross-Reference Version (KJV)

3. Say it

4. Pray it

2:1-2

Prayer to Jesus

Thanksgiving

Commitment

Jesus' Response

Creative Worship

Song 2:3-4

³ As the apple tree among the trees of the wood, so is my beloved among the sons. I sat down under his shadow with great delight, and his fruit was sweet to my taste. ⁴ He brought me to the banqueting house, and his banner over me was love.

date

1. Read it

2. Write it

Alternate Bible Version

Personal Paraphrase Version (NIV)

Key Words

Questions

Insights

Cross-Reference Version (KJV)

3. Say it

4. Pray it

2:3-4

Prayer to Jesus

Thanksgiving

Commitment

Jesus' Response

Creative Worship

Song 2:5-6

date

1. Read it

2. Write it

⁵ Stay me with flagons,
comfort me with apples:
for I am sick of love.
⁶ His left hand is
under my head, and
his right hand
doth embrace me.

Alternate Bible Version

Personal Paraphrase Version (PPV)

Key Words

Questions

Insights

Cross-Reference Version (KJV)

3. Say it

4. Pray it

2:5-6

Prayer to Jesus

Thanksgiving

Commitment

Jesus' Response

Creative Worship

Song 2:7

date _____

1. Read it

2. Write it

[7] I charge you, O ye daughters
of Jerusalem, by the roes,
and by the hinds of the field,
that ye stir not up,
nor awake my love,
till he please.

Alternate Bible Version

_____

_____

_____

_____

_____

Personal Paraphrase Version (PPV)

_____

_____

_____

_____

_____

_____

_____

Key Words

Questions

Insights

Cross-Reference Version (KJV)

3. Say it

4. Pray it

2:7

Prayer to Jesus

Thanksgiving

Commitment

Jesus' Response

Creative Worship

Song 2:8-9

8 The voice of my beloved! behold, he cometh leaping upon the mountains, skipping upon the hills. 9 My beloved is like a roe or a young hart: behold, he standeth behind our wall, he looketh forth at the windows, shewing himself through the lattice.

date

1. Read it

2. Write it

Alternate Bible Version

Personal Paraphrase Version (PPV)

Key Words

Questions

Insights

Cross-Reference Version (KJV)

3. Say it

4. Pray it

2:8-9

Prayer to Jesus

Thanksgiving

Commitment

Jesus' Response

Creative Worship

Song 2:10-12

¹⁰ My beloved spake, and said unto me, Rise up, my love, my fair one, and come away. ¹¹ For, lo, the winter is past, the rain is over and gone; ¹² The flowers appear on the earth; the time of the singing of birds is come, and the voice of the turtle is heard in our land;

date

1. Read it

2. Write it

Alternate Bible Version

Personal Paraphrase Version (PPV)

Key Words

Questions

Insights

Cross-Reference Version (KJV)

3. Say it

4. Pray it

2:10-12

Prayer to Jesus

Thanksgiving

Commitment

Jesus' Response

Creative Worship

Song 2:13-14

¹³ The fig tree putteth forth her green figs, and the vines with the tender grape give a good smell. Arise, my love, my fair one, and come away. ¹⁴ O my dove, that art in the clefts of the rock, in the secret places of the stairs, let me see thy countenance, let me hear thy voice; for sweet is thy voice, and thy countenance is comely.

date

1. Read it

2. Write it

Alternate Bible Version

Personal Paraphrase Version (PPV)

Key Words

Questions

Insights

Cross-Reference Version (KJV)

3. Say it

4. Pray it

2:13-14

Prayer to Jesus

Thanksgiving

Commitment

Jesus' Response

Creative Worship

Song 2:15-16

¹⁵ Take us the foxes, the little foxes, that spoil the vines: for our vines have tender grapes. ¹⁶ My beloved is mine, and I am his: he feedeth among the lilies.

date

1. Read it

2. Write it

Alternate Bible Version

Personal Paraphrase Version (PPV)

Key Words

Questions

Insights

Cross-Reference Version (CRV)

3. Say it

4. Pray it

2:15-16

Prayer to Jesus

Thanksgiving

Commitment

Jesus' Response

Creative Worship

Journey through the Song of Solomon

Song 2:17

date

1. Read it

2. Write it

Alternate Bible Version

Personal Paraphrase Version (PPV)

¹⁷ Until the day break,
and the shadows flee away,
turn, my beloved,
and be thou like a roe
or a young hart
upon the mountains
of Bether.

Key Words

Questions

Insights

Cross-Reference Version (KJV)

3. Say it

4. Pray it

2:17

Prayer to Jesus

Thanksgiving

Commitment

Jesus' Response

Creative Worship

Song of Solomon | 3

¹ By night on my bed I sought him whom my soul loveth: I sought him, but I found him not. ² I will rise now, and go about the city in the streets, and in the broad ways I will seek him whom my soul loveth: I sought him, but I found him not. ³ The watchmen that go about the city found me: to whom I said, Saw ye him whom my soul loveth? ⁴ It was but a little that I passed from them, but I found him whom my soul loveth: I held him, and would not let him go, until I had brought him into my mother's house, and into the chamber of her that conceived me. ⁵ I charge you, O ye daughters of Jerusalem, by the roes, and by the hinds of the field, that ye stir not up, nor awake my love, till he please. ⁶ Who is this that cometh out of the wilderness like pillars of smoke, perfumed with myrrh and frankincense, with all powders of the merchant? ⁷ Behold his bed, which is Solomon's; threescore valiant men are about it, of the valiant of Israel. ⁸ They all hold swords, being expert in war: every man hath his sword upon his thigh because of fear in the night. ⁹ King Solomon made himself a chariot of the wood of Lebanon. ¹⁰ He made the pillars thereof of silver, the bottom thereof of gold, the covering of it of purple, the midst thereof being paved with love, for the daughters of Jerusalem. ¹¹ Go forth, O ye daughters of Zion, and behold king Solomon with the crown wherewith his mother crowned him in the day of his espousals, and in the day of the gladness of his heart.

Chapter Three Overview

Jesus withdraws His tangible presence from us temporarily in order to cultivate longing in our hearts for Him. He has drawn us to Himself in extravagant worship and invited us into Bridal partnership. Now is the time for us to begin running with Him in ministry. We experience the loving chastisement of our Heavenly Father until we arise to follow Jesus realizing that our hearts are only safe in the context of one hundred percent obedience. As our Father, God is committed to bringing each of us forth as a glorious mature Bride for His Son, Jesus Christ.

The Holy Spirit reveals Jesus as the **Safe Savior** who ensures our arrival upon the great Wedding Day through His own intercession and provision. The royal procession is surrounded by a mighty army. The Lord will finish the good work He started in us (Phil. 1:6). His own zeal will perform it. His incarnation, death, and resurrection prove His goodness. With excitement we begin to teach other believers our newfound discoveries. We exhort them to press into Jesus in light of His glorious redemption and excellent leadership. This significant revelation prepares us for a great turning point in our commitment to Jesus.

We are no longer afraid to leave the comfort zone because we believe our hearts will be secure. We know that obedience will bring life and eternal joy, not death. Because earthly authority figures are not always trustworthy, we have believed the enemy's lies about Jesus, our ultimate authority. We can only see Him as safe from the viewpoint of eternity. He is omniscient. He sees the end from the beginning and knows how to lead us. This is the key to trusting God in every circumstance. Our new depth of commitment flows out of this insight into the Lord's loving leadership.

There will be a day when the Church from throughout history will crown Jesus as King. The final triumph is described in Revelation 19:1-16 as the Wedding Day between Jesus Christ and His Bride, the Church. Jesus will receive His mature Bride with the gladness of a Bridegroom (Is. 62:5). We will likewise rejoice with all of heaven (Rev. 19:6).

Song 3:1-2

date

1. Read it

¹ By night on my bed I sought him whom my
soul loveth: I sought him, but I found him not.
² I will rise now, and go about the city in
the streets, and in the broad ways
I will seek him whom my soul loveth:
I sought him, but I found him not.

2. Write it

Alternate Bible Version

Personal Paraphrase Version (PPV)

Key Words

Questions

Insights

Cross-Reference Version (CRV)

3. Say it

4. Pray it

3:1-2

Prayer to Jesus

Thanksgiving

Commitment

Jesus' Response

Creative Worship

Song 3:3-4

³ The watchmen that go about the city found me:
to whom I said, Saw ye him whom my soul loveth?
⁴ It was but a little that I passed from them,
but I found him whom my soul loveth:
I held him, and would not let him go,
until I had brought him into
my mother's house, and into the
chamber of her that conceived me.

date

1. Read it

2. Write it

Alternate Bible Version

Personal Paraphrase Version (PPV)

Key Words

Questions

Insights

Cross-Reference Version (CRV)

3. Say it

4. Pray it

3:3-4

Prayer to Jesus

Thanksgiving

Commitment

Jesus' Response

Creative Worship

Song 3:5

⁵ I charge you, O ye daughters of Jerusalem, by the roes, and by the hinds of the field, that ye stir not up, nor awake my love, till he please.

date

1. Read it

2. Write it

Alternate Bible Version

Personal Paraphrase Version (PPV)

Key Words

Questions

Insights

Cross-Reference Version (CRV)

3. Say it

4. Pray it

3:5

Prayer to Jesus

Thanksgiving

Commitment

Jesus' Response

Creative Worship

Song 3:6

⁶ Who is this that cometh
out of the wilderness
like pillars of smoke,
perfumed with myrrh
and frankincense,
with all powders
of the merchant?

date

1. Read it

2. Write it

Alternate Bible Version

Personal Paraphrase Version (PPV)

Key Words

Questions

Insights

Cross-Reference Version (KJV)

3. Say it

4. Pray it

3:6

Prayer to Jesus

Thanksgiving

Commitment

Jesus' Response

Creative Worship

Song 3:7-8

date

1. Read it

2. Write it

[7] Behold his bed, which is Solomon's; threescore valiant men are about it, of the valiant of Israel. [8] They all hold swords, being expert in war: every man hath his sword upon his thigh because of fear in the night.

Alternate Bible Version

_____

_____

_____

_____

Personal Paraphrase Version (PPV)

_____

_____

_____

_____

_____

_____

Key Words

Questions

Insights

Cross-Reference Version (CRV)

3. Say it

4. Pray it

3:7-8

Prayer to Jesus

Thanksgiving

Commitment

Jesus' Response

Creative Worship

Song 3:9-10

date

1. Read it

2. Write it

⁹ King Solomon made himself a chariot of the wood of Lebanon. ¹⁰ He made the pillars thereof of silver, the bottom thereof of gold, the covering of it of purple, the midst thereof being paved with love, for the daughters of Jerusalem.

Alternate Bible Version

Personal Paraphrase Version (PPV)

Key Words

Questions

Insights

Cross-Reference Version (KJV)

3. Say it

4. Pray it

3:9-10

Prayer to Jesus

Thanksgiving

Commitment

Jesus' Response

Creative Worship

Song 3:11

¹¹ Go forth, O ye daughters of Zion,
and behold king Solomon with the crown
wherewith his mother crowned him
in the day of his espousals,
and in the day of the gladness
of his heart.

date

1. Read it

2. Write it

Alternate Bible Version

Personal Paraphrase Version (PPV)

Key Words

Questions

Insights

Cross-Reference Version (CRV)

3. Say it

4. Pray it

3:11

Prayer to Jesus

Thanksgiving

Commitment

Jesus' Response

Creative Worship

Song of Solomon | 4

¹ Behold, thou art fair, my love; behold, thou art fair; thou hast doves' eyes within thy locks: thy hair is as a flock of goats, that appear from mount Gilead. ² Thy teeth are like a flock of sheep that are even shorn, which came up from the washing; whereof every one bear twins, and none is barren among them. ³ Thy lips are like a thread of scarlet, and thy speech is comely: thy temples are like a piece of a pomegranate within thy locks. ⁴ Thy neck is like the tower of David builded for an armoury, whereon there hang a thousand bucklers, all shields of mighty men. ⁵ Thy two breasts are like two young roes that are twins, which feed among the lilies. ⁶ Until the day break, and the shadows flee away, I will get me to the mountain of myrrh, and to the hill of frankincense. ⁷ Thou art all fair, my love; there is no spot in thee. ⁸ Come with me from Lebanon, my spouse, with me from Lebanon: look from the top of Amana, from the top of Shenir and Hermon, from the lions' dens, from the mountains of the leopards. ⁹ Thou hast ravished my heart, my sister, my spouse; thou hast ravished my heart with one of thine eyes, with one chain of thy neck. ¹⁰ How fair is thy love, my sister, my spouse! how much better is thy love than wine! and the smell of thine ointments than all spices! ¹¹ Thy lips, O my spouse, drop as the honeycomb: honey and milk are under thy tongue; and the smell of thy garments is like the smell of Lebanon. ¹² A garden inclosed is my sister, my spouse; a spring shut up, a fountain sealed. ¹³ Thy plants are an orchard of pomegranates, with pleasant fruits; camphire, with spikenard, ¹⁴ Spikenard and saffron; calamus and cinnamon, with all trees of frankincense; myrrh and aloes, with all the chief spices: ¹⁵ A fountain of gardens, a well of living waters, and streams from Lebanon. ¹⁶ Awake, O north wind; and come, thou south; blow upon my garden, that the spices thereof may flow out. Let my beloved come into his garden, and eat his pleasant fruits.

Chapter Four Overview

Jesus, our **Heavenly Bridegroom,** breaks the silence with cherishing words. These are the first words He speaks to us after withdrawing His presence in a season of Divine chastisement. He begins by prophetically affirming eight budding virtues in our lives – characteristics that exist only in small form, which He will bring forth as we seek to fearlessly obey Him. God uses this strategy of affirmation to equip us for spiritual warfare against all of Satan's accusations. He cherishes us as weak believers that we may become His mature Bride. This aspect of the Holy Spirit's ministry may be difficult to receive if we have been weighed down by religious doctrine that conveys God is stoic concerning us.

The symbolism used here is developed throughout the Scripture. 'Dove's eyes' speak of devoted faith and revelation. 'Hair like goats' signifies dedication to God and spiritual submission. 'Teeth like shorn sheep' indicates nourishment that comes by chewing and meditating on the meat of the Word. 'Lips like scarlet' refers to speech that is influenced by redemption. The 'mouth' reveals intimate communion with God. 'Veiled temples' describes our emotions that have been impacted by God's. 'Neck like David's tower' portrays our free will. 'Breasts like fawns' illustrates our ability to edify and nurture others. Such declaration of passionate affection empowers us to commit to the Lord in total obedience as we embrace the Cross and follow our tailor made paths to become like Him.

Jesus is a passionate Bridegroom committed to winning our hearts. He reveals His desire for us and romances us by declaring the truth of our identity as His eternal Bride. As we drink from the well of Living Water and abide daily in Him we become flourishing gardens with godly lives and fruitful ministries (John 4:14; 7:37-38; 15:5).

Fully confident in God's love for us we can more readily invite His north winds of testing and south winds of blessing to transform us. We give our entire lives to the Lord in order to become His fragrance and spread the testimony of Jesus to the nations. We want Him to receive the fullness of His inheritance. This is a major turning point in our journey.

Song 4:1-2

¹ Behold, thou art fair, my love; behold, thou art fair; thou hast doves' eyes within thy locks: thy hair is as a flock of goats, that appear from mount Gilead. ² Thy teeth are like a flock of sheep that are even shorn, which came up from the washing; whereof every one bear twins, and none is barren among them.

date

1. Read it

2. Write it

Alternate Bible Version

Personal Paraphrase Version (PPV)

Key Words

Questions

Insights

Cross-Reference Version (CRV)

3. Say it

4. Pray it

4:1-2

Prayer to Jesus

Thanksgiving

Commitment

Jesus' Response

Creative Worship

Song 4:3-5

date

1. Read it

³ Thy lips are like a thread of scarlet, and thy speech is comely: thy temples are like a piece of a pomegranate within thy locks. ⁴ Thy neck is like the tower of David builded for an armoury, whereon there hang a thousand bucklers, all shields of mighty men. ⁵ Thy two breasts are like two young roes that are twins, which feed among the lilies.

2. Write it

Alternate Bible Version

_____

_____

_____

_____

Personal Paraphrase Version (PPV)

_____

_____

_____

_____

_____

_____

Key Words

Questions

Insights

Cross-Reference Version (CRV)

3. Say it

4. Pray it

4:3-5

Prayer to Jesus

Thanksgiving

Commitment

Jesus' Response

Creative Worship

Song 4:6

⁶ Until the day break, and the shadows flee away, I will get me to the mountain of myrrh, and to the hill of frankincense.

date

1. Read it

2. Write it

Alternate Bible Version

Personal Paraphrase Version (PPV)

Key Words

Questions

Insights

Cross-Reference Version (KJV)

3. Say it

4. Pray it

4:6

Prayer to Jesus

Thanksgiving

Commitment

Jesus' Response

Creative Worship

Song 4:7-8

date

7 Thou art all fair, my love; there is no spot in thee. 8 Come with me from Lebanon, my spouse, with me from Lebanon: look from the top of Amana, from the top of Shenir and Hermon, from the lions' dens, from the mountains of the leopards.

1. Read it

2. Write it

Alternate Bible Version

Personal Paraphrase Version (PPV)

Key Words

Questions

Insights

Cross-Reference Version (KJV)

3. Say it

4. Pray it

4:7-8

Prayer to Jesus

Thanksgiving

Commitment

Jesus' Response

Creative Worship

Song 4:9-10

⁹ Thou hast ravished my heart, my sister, my spouse; thou hast ravished my heart with one of thine eyes, with one chain of thy neck. ¹⁰ How fair is thy love, my sister, my spouse! how much better is thy love than wine! and the smell of thine ointments than all spices!

date

1. Read it

2. Write it

Alternate Bible Version

Personal Paraphrase Version (PPV)

Key Words

Questions

Insights

Cross-Reference Version (KJV)

3. Say it

4. Pray it

4:9-10

Prayer to Jesus

Thanksgiving

Commitment

Jesus' Response

Creative Worship

Song 4:11

¹¹ Thy lips, O my spouse,
drop as the honeycomb:
honey and milk are
under thy tongue;
and the smell
of thy garments
is like the smell
of Lebanon.

date

1. Read it

2. Write it

Alternate Bible Version

Personal Paraphrase Version (ppv)

Key Words

Questions

Insights

Cross-Reference Version (KJV)

3. Say it

4. Pray it

4:11

Prayer to Jesus

Thanksgiving

Commitment

Jesus' Response

Creative Worship

Song 4:12-15

date

1. Read it

2. Write it

¹² A garden inclosed is my sister, my spouse; a spring shut up, a fountain sealed. ¹³ Thy plants are an orchard of pomegranates, with pleasant fruits; camphire, with spikenard, ¹⁴ Spikenard and saffron; calamus and cinnamon, with all trees of frankincense; myrrh and aloes, with all the chief spices: ¹⁵ A fountain of gardens, a well of living waters, and streams from Lebanon.

Alternate Bible Version

Personal Paraphrase Version (PPV)

Key Words

Questions

Insights

Cross-Reference Version (KJV)

3. Say it

4. Pray it

4:12-15

Prayer to Jesus

Thanksgiving

Commitment

Jesus' Response

Creative Worship

Song 4:16

date

¹⁶ Awake, O north wind; and come, thou south; blow upon my garden, that the spices thereof may flow out. Let my beloved come into his garden, and eat his pleasant fruits.

1. Read it

2. Write it

Alternate Bible Version

Personal Paraphrase Version (PPV)

Key Words

Questions

Insights

Cross-Reference Version (CRV)

3. Say it

4. Pray it

4:16

Prayer to Jesus

Thanksgiving

Commitment

Jesus' Response

Creative Worship

Song of Solomon | 5

¹ I am come into my garden, my sister, my spouse: I have gathered my myrrh with my spice; I have eaten my honeycomb with my honey; I have drunk my wine with my milk: eat, O friends; drink, yea, drink abundantly, O beloved. ² I sleep, but my heart waketh: it is the voice of my beloved that knocketh, saying, Open to me, my sister, my love, my dove, my undefiled: for my head is filled with dew, and my locks with the drops of the night. ³ I have put off my coat; how shall I put it on? I have washed my feet; how shall I defile them? ⁴ My beloved put in his hand by the hole of the door, and my bowels were moved for him. ⁵ I rose up to open to my beloved; and my hands dropped with myrrh, and my fingers with sweet smelling myrrh, upon the handles of the lock. ⁶ I opened to my beloved; but my beloved had withdrawn himself, and was gone: my soul failed when he spake: I sought him, but I could not find him; I called him, but he gave me no answer. ⁷ The watchmen that went about the city found me, they smote me, they wounded me; the keepers of the walls took away my veil from me. ⁸ I charge you, O daughters of Jerusalem, if ye find my beloved, that ye tell him, that I am sick of love. ⁹ What is thy beloved more than another beloved, O thou fairest among women? what is thy beloved more than another beloved, that thou dost so charge us? ¹⁰ My beloved is white and ruddy, the chiefest among ten thousand. ¹¹ His head is as the most fine gold, his locks are bushy, and black as a raven. ¹² His eyes are as the eyes of doves by the rivers of waters, washed with milk, and fitly set. ¹³ His cheeks are as a bed of spices, as sweet flowers: his lips like lilies, dropping sweet smelling myrrh. ¹⁴ His hands are as gold rings set with the beryl: his belly is as bright ivory overlaid with sapphires. ¹⁵ His legs are as pillars of marble, set upon sockets of fine gold: his countenance is as Lebanon, excellent as the cedars. ¹⁶ His mouth is most sweet: yea, he is altogether lovely. This is my beloved, and this is my friend, O daughters of Jerusalem.

Chapter Five Overview

Jesus answers our prayers for the north and south winds by taking full possession of us as His inheritance. This is a pivotal chapter in the Song. The focus shifts from our inheritance in Jesus to His inheritance in us. We want to love Jesus as He loves us in order to become the Father's gift to His Son (Eph. 1:18).

The Lord knows the best combination of adversity and blessing suitable to bring each individual believer into full maturity and partnership. He appears as the **Suffering Servant** with the bitter north winds. Christ, who suffered alone in the garden, now beckons to us, "Come with Me to Gethsemane." Jesus embraced the Cross for the joy set before Him and invites us to take up our Cross, follow Him, and share in the fellowship of His sufferings (Heb. 12:2; Matt. 16:24; Phil. 3:10).

Earlier Jesus withdrew His manifest presence to discipline us as a result of disobedience. Now He withdraws His presence to test our faithfulness in difficult circumstances. This usually involves relational disruption. The Lord may allow spiritual authorities in the Body of Christ to misunderstand us, wound us unjustly, and take away our places of function in the Church. This 'dark night of the soul' is our ultimate test of maturity. Our inheritance — feeling God's nearness (intimacy) and serving with Him in ministry (partnership) — seems so distant. It appears as though all of His promises have vanished. In reality we stand vulnerable before God. The test is clear. Will we become offended at the Lord for withdrawing His presence and allowing us to be so severely mistreated, or will we respond with greater passion for Jesus? We must respond in love and humility.

This is an opportunity to turn our pain into worship as we declare the beauty and faithfulness of our **Majestic God**. He is our faithful friend. Hearts overflowing with love for Jesus can boldly withstand the enemy's constant temptations to 'curse God and die' (Job 2:9). When others accuse God for abandoning and wounding us we can proclaim the truth of Jesus' perfect leadership in our lives. This testimony will actually launch us into greater intimacy with God and ministry to people.

Song 5:1

¹ I am come into my garden, my sister, my spouse:
I have gathered my myrrh with my spice;
I have eaten my honeycomb with my honey;
I have drunk my wine with my milk:
eat, O friends; drink,
yea, drink abundantly,
O beloved.

date

1. Read it

2. Write it

Alternate Bible Version

_____

_____

_____

_____

_____

Personal Paraphrase Version (PPV)

_____

_____

_____

_____

_____

_____

_____

Key Words

Questions

Insights

Cross-Reference Version (KJV)

3. Say it

4. Pray it

5:1

Prayer to Jesus

Thanksgiving

Commitment

Jesus' Response

Creative Worship

Song 5:2-3

date

1. Read it

2. Write it

² I sleep, but my heart waketh: it is the voice of
my beloved that knocketh, saying, Open to me,
my sister, my love, my dove, my undefiled:
for my head is filled with dew, and my locks
with the drops of the night. ³ I have put
off my coat; how shall I put it on?
I have washed my feet;
how shall I defile them?

Alternate Bible Version

Personal Paraphrase Version (PPV)

Key Words

Questions

Insights

Cross-Reference Version (KJV)

3. Say it

4. Pray it

5:2-3

Prayer to Jesus

Thanksgiving

Commitment

Jesus' Response

Creative Worship

Song 5:4-5

⁴ My beloved put in his hand by the hole of the door, and my bowels were moved for him. ⁵ I rose up to open to my beloved; and my hands dropped with myrrh, and my fingers with sweet smelling myrrh, upon the handles of the lock.

date

1. Read it

2. Write it

Alternate Bible Version

Personal Paraphrase Version (PPV)

Key Words

Questions

Insights

Cross-Reference Version (KJV)

3. Say it

4. Pray it

5:4-5

Prayer to Jesus

Thanksgiving

Commitment

Jesus' Response

Creative Worship

Song 5:6

⁶ I opened to my beloved; but my beloved had withdrawn himself, and was gone: my soul failed when he spake: I sought him, but I could not find him; I called him, but he gave me no answer.

date

1. Read it

2. Write it

Alternate Bible Version

Personal Paraphrase Version (PPV)

Key Words

Questions

Insights

Cross-Reference Version (KJV)

3. Say it

4. Pray it

5:6

Prayer to Jesus

Thanksgiving

Commitment

Jesus' Response

Creative Worship

Song 5:7

date

⁷ The watchmen that went about
the city found me, they smote
me, they wounded me;
the keepers of the walls
took away my veil from me.

1. Read it

2. Write it

Alternate Bible Version

Personal Paraphrase Version (PPV)

Key Words

Questions

Insights

Cross-Reference Version (KJV)

3. Say it

4. Pray it

5:7

Prayer to Jesus

Thanksgiving

Commitment

Jesus' Response

Creative Worship

Song 5:8-9

date

1. Read it

2. Write it

⁸ I charge you, O daughters of Jerusalem, if ye find my beloved, that ye tell him, that I am sick of love. ⁹ What is thy beloved more than another beloved, O thou fairest among women? what is thy beloved more than another beloved, that thou dost so charge us?

Alternate Bible Version

Personal Paraphrase Version (PPV)

Key Words

Questions

Insights

Cross-Reference Version (KJV)

3. Say it

4. Pray it

5:8-9

Prayer to Jesus

Thanksgiving

Commitment

Jesus' Response

Creative Worship

Song 5:10-13

date

1. Read it

¹⁰ My beloved is white and ruddy, the chiefest among ten thousand. ¹¹ His head is as the most fine gold, his locks are bushy, and black as a raven. ¹² His eyes are as the eyes of doves by the rivers of waters, washed with milk, and fitly set. ¹³ His cheeks are as a bed of spices, as sweet flowers: his lips like lilies, dropping sweet smelling myrrh.

2. Write it

Alternate Bible Version

_____

_____

_____

_____

_____

Personal Paraphrase Version (PPV)

_____

_____

_____

_____

_____

_____

_____

Key Words

Questions

Insights

Cross-Reference Version (KJV)

3. Say it

4. Pray it

5:10-13

Creative Worship

Song 5:14-16

¹⁴ His hands are as gold rings set with the beryl: his belly is as bright ivory overlaid with sapphires. ¹⁵ His legs are as pillars of marble, set upon sockets of fine gold: his countenance is as Lebanon, excellent as the cedars. ¹⁶ His mouth is most sweet: yea, he is altogether lovely. This is my beloved, and this is my friend, O daughters of Jerusalem.

date

1. Read it

2. Write it

Alternate Bible Version

Personal Paraphrase Version (PPV)

Key Words

Questions

Insights

Cross-Reference Version (CRV)

3. Say it

4. Pray it

5:14-16

Prayer to Jesus

Thanksgiving

Commitment

Jesus' Response

Creative Worship

Song of Solomon 6

¹ Whither is thy beloved gone, O thou fairest among women? whither is thy beloved turned aside? that we may seek him with thee. ² My beloved is gone down into his garden, to the beds of spices, to feed in the gardens, and to gather lilies. ³ I am my beloved's, and my beloved is mine: he feedeth among the lilies. ⁴ Thou art beautiful, O my love, as Tirzah, comely as Jerusalem, terrible as an army with banners. ⁵ Turn away thine eyes from me, for they have overcome me: thy hair is as a flock of goats that appear from Gilead. ⁶ Thy teeth are as a flock of sheep which go up from the washing, whereof every one beareth twins, and there is not one barren among them. ⁷ As a piece of a pomegranate are thy temples within thy locks. ⁸ There are threescore queens, and fourscore concubines, and virgins without number. ⁹ My dove, my undefiled is but one; she is the only one of her mother, she is the choice one of her that bare her. The daughters saw her, and blessed her; yea, the queens and the concubines, and they praised her. ¹⁰ Who is she that looketh forth as the morning, fair as the moon, clear as the sun, and terrible as an army with banners? ¹¹ I went down into the garden of nuts to see the fruits of the valley, and to see whether the vine flourished and the pomegranates budded. ¹² Or ever I was aware, my soul made me like the chariots of Amminadib. ¹³ Return, return, O Shulamite; return, return, that we may look upon thee. What will ye see in the Shulamite? As it were the company of two armies.

Chapter Six Overview

Lovesick responses during the 'dark night' of our souls will provoke other believers to ask, "How can we know Jesus intimately like you do?" We can then teach these 'daughters' how to mature in intimacy with the Lord by sharing what we have learned from our experiences. Young believers will glean from our lives as we encourage them to feed on the beauty of Jesus in the Word of God. In this way, we begin to partner with the Lord in gathering souls for the Great Harvest.

Jesus returns His manifest presence and breaks this second season of silence. In His evaluation of our struggle He says, "My Beloved, you have prevailed. In the great test you have come forth victoriously." The trials now seem worth all the pain. With one of the greatest statements in God's Word, Jesus declares that our eyes of loving devotion overcome Him. He celebrates the marvelous beauty imparted to us by the Holy Spirit through tribulation. It is not even worth comparing our sufferings with the beauty and glory that will be revealed in us in eternity (Rom. 8:18). Our beauty is the fruit produced by Divine testing, obedient responses, and revelation of the Lord's affections.

Repeating descriptive phrases from chapter four Jesus tells us, "Your dedication is powerful. You have matured in your ability to live by the meat of My Word." He continues to praise our beauty by honoring us above all the royal hosts in the eternal city. We each capture the heart of our Bridegroom in a unique way. We are His Bride, His favorite one!

Believers also esteem our spiritual maturity. Even the host of heaven rejoices with eternal gladness as we step into our position as Christ's Bride. Three increasing stages of light depict our progression into the glory of God. Ultimately, we conquer all darkness in our hearts and triumph over the enemy through our authority in Christ Jesus.

With such victory in our lives we are overcome with love, concern, and desire for the whole Church. As we enter the 'promised land' of Bridal partnership, whether we encounter sincere and sarcastic responses from the Body of Christ, our loyalty to God must remain steadfast.

Song 6:1

date

¹ Whither is thy beloved gone,
O thou fairest among women?
whither is thy beloved
turned aside?
that we may seek
him with thee.

1. Read it

2. Write it

Alternate Bible Version

_____
_____
_____
_____
_____

Personal Paraphrase Version (PPV)

_____
_____
_____
_____
_____
_____

Key Words

Questions

Insights

Cross-Reference Version (KJV)

3. Say it

4. Pray it

6:1

Prayer to Jesus

Thanksgiving

Commitment

Jesus' Response

Creative Worship

Song 6:2-3

date

1. Read it

2. Write it

² My beloved is gone down into his garden, to the beds of spices, to feed in the gardens, and to gather lilies. ³ I am my beloved's, and my beloved is mine: he feedeth among the lilies.

Alternate Bible Version

Personal Paraphrase Version (PPV)

Journey through the Song of Solomon

Key Words

Questions

Insights

Cross-Reference Version (CRV)

3. Say it

4. Pray it

6:2-3

Prayer to Jesus

Thanksgiving

Commitment

Jesus' Response

Creative Worship

Song 6:4

⁴ Thou art beautiful, O my love, as Tirzah,
comely as Jerusalem, terrible as
an army with banners.

date

1. Read it

2. Write it

Alternate Bible Version

_____

_____

_____

_____

_____

Personal Paraphrase Version (PPV)

_____

_____

_____

_____

_____

_____

Key Words

Questions

Insights

Cross-Reference Version (KJV)

3. Say it

4. Pray it

6:4

Prayer to Jesus

Thanksgiving

Commitment

Jesus' Response

Creative Worship

Song 6:5-7

date

1. Read it

⁵ Turn away thine eyes from me, for they have overcome me: thy hair is as a flock of goats that appear from Gilead. ⁶ Thy teeth are as a flock of sheep which go up from the washing, whereof every one beareth twins, and there is not one barren among them. ⁷ As a piece of a pomegranate are thy temples within thy locks.

2. Write it

Alternate Bible Version

Personal Paraphrase Version (PPV)

Key Words

Questions

Insights

Cross-Reference Version (KJV)

3. Say it

4. Pray it

6:5-7

Prayer to Jesus

Thanksgiving

Commitment

Jesus' Response

Creative Worship

Song 6:8-9

⁸ There are threescore queens, and fourscore concubines, and virgins without number. ⁹ My dove, my undefiled is but one; she is the only one of her mother, she is the choice one of her that bare her. The daughters saw her, and blessed her; yea, the queens and the concubines, and they praised her.

date

1. Read it

2. Write it

Alternate Bible Version

Personal Paraphrase Version (PPV)

Key Words

Questions

Insights

Cross-Reference Version (KJV)

3. Say it

4. Pray it

6:8-9

Prayer to Jesus

Thanksgiving

Commitment

Jesus' Response

Creative Worship

Song 6:10-12

date

1. Read it

¹⁰ Who is she that looketh forth as the morning, fair as the moon, clear as the sun, and terrible as an army with banners? ¹¹ I went down into the garden of nuts to see the fruits of the valley, and to see whether the vine flourished, and the pomegranates budded. ¹² Or ever I was aware, my soul made me like the chariots of Amminadib.

2. Write it

Alternate Bible Version

Personal Paraphrase Version (PPV)

Key Words

Questions

Insights

Cross-Reference Version (KJV)

3. Say it

4. Pray it

6:10-12

Prayer to Jesus

Thanksgiving

Commitment

Jesus' Response

Creative Worship

Song 6:13

date

1. Read it

2. Write it

¹³ Return, return, O Shulamite; return, return, that we may look upon thee. What will ye see in the Shulamite? As it were the company of two armies.

Alternate Bible Version

Personal Paraphrase Version

Key Words

Questions

Insights

Cross-Reference Version (KJV)

3. Say it

4. Pray it

6:13

Prayer to Jesus

Thanksgiving

Commitment

Jesus' Response

Creative Worship

Song of Solomon | 7

¹ How beautiful are thy feet with shoes, O prince's daughter! the joints of thy thighs are like jewels, the work of the hands of a cunning workman. ² Thy navel is like a round goblet, which wanteth not liquor: thy belly is like an heap of wheat set about with lilies. ³ Thy two breasts are like two young roes that are twins. ⁴ Thy neck is as a tower of ivory; thine eyes like the fishpools in Heshbon, by the gate of Bathrabbim: thy nose is as the tower of Lebanon which looketh toward Damascus. ⁵ Thine head upon thee is like Carmel, and the hair of thine head like purple; the king is held in the galleries. ⁶ How fair and how pleasant art thou, O love, for delights! ⁷ This thy stature is like to a palm tree, and thy breasts to clusters of grapes. ⁸ I said, I will go up to the palm tree, I will take hold of the boughs thereof: now also thy breasts shall be as clusters of the vine, and the smell of thy nose like apples; ⁹ And the roof of thy mouth like the best wine for my beloved, that goeth down sweetly, causing the lips of those that are asleep to speak. ¹⁰ I am my beloved's, and his desire is toward me. ¹¹ Come, my beloved, let us go forth into the field; let us lodge in the villages. ¹² Let us get up early to the vineyards; let us see if the vine flourish, whether the tender grape appear, and the pomegranates bud forth: there will I give thee my loves. ¹³ The mandrakes give a smell, and at our gates are all manner of pleasant fruits, new and old, which I have laid up for thee, O my beloved.

Chapter Seven Overview

In this season we are first vindicated by those who praise our spiritual beauty. The Church is compelled by our effectiveness in evangelism as depicted by our feet in sandals. 'Prince's daughter' emphasizes our royal character and inner lives as the King's Bride (Ps. 45:13; Rev. 21:9). God's grace adorns us. He nourishes us with healthy spiritual diets that enable us to impart to others. Discerning saints see that we are about to reap a harvest. We are equipped to nurture, edify, and reproduce life in the Kingdom of God. Our lives are completely submitted to the will of the Lord. The eyes of our understanding are now enlightened with spiritual wisdom and revelation (Eph. 1:17-18). Others are protected by our ability to discern spiritual enemies. We take our thoughts captive in obedience to Christ so our minds are not vulnerable to Satan's attacks (2 Cor. 10:5). Our hearts are filled with holy resolve to obey God even under pressure.

The Lord also vindicates us by releasing anointing to endorse us as His partners. Jesus commissions us to nurture people, impart the Holy Spirit, and maintain lives of intimacy with Him. The Lord's heart is captivated by our devotion as we embrace His Greatest Commandment of loving God wholly and His Great Commission of discipling nations. The Father has promised to give Jesus the nations as His inheritance (Ps. 2:8). Jesus wants His Bride to participate with Him in this Great Harvest of souls. We do so by drinking the cup of His will without hindrance. At the beginning of our journey we were burned out from laboring without love. Now, as a result of God's restoration, we want to labor with Him in His vineyards.

The Lord takes great delight in the abundance of fruit produced from our lives of intimacy and partnership with Him. We are Jesus' inheritance. He deeply desires ongoing intimate communion with each of us. Our Bridal partnership is now expressed in mature obedience to Jesus and continual intercession. Love for our Beloved, Jesus Christ, now motivates us to engage in spiritual warfare against the enemy's schemes.

Song 7:1

date

1. Read it

2. Write it

¹ How beautiful are thy feet with shoes, O prince's daughter! the joints of thy thighs are like jewels, the work of the hands of a cunning workman.

Alternate Bible Version

Personal Paraphrase Version (PPV)

Key Words

Questions

Insights

Cross-Reference Version (KJV)

3. Say it

4. Pray it

7:1

Prayer to Jesus

Thanksgiving

Commitment

Jesus' Response

Creative Worship

Song 7:2-4

² Thy navel is like a round goblet, which wanteth not liquor: thy belly is like an heap of wheat set about with lilies. ³ Thy two breasts are like two young roes that are twins. ⁴ Thy neck is as a tower of ivory; thine eyes like the fishpools in Heshbon, by the gate of Bathrabbim: thy nose is as the tower of Lebanon which looketh toward Damascus.

date

1. Read it

2. Write it

Alternate Bible Version

Personal Paraphrase Version (PPV)

Key Words

Questions

Insights

Cross-Reference Version (KJV)

3. Say it

4. Pray it

7:2-4

Prayer to Jesus

Thanksgiving

Commitment

Jesus' Response

Creative Worship

Song 7:5-6

date

1. Read it

2. Write it

⁵ Thine head upon thee is like Carmel, and the hair of thine head like purple; the king is held in the galleries. ⁶ How fair and how pleasant art thou, O love, for delights!

Alternate Bible Version

Personal Paraphrase Version (PPV)

Key Words

Questions

Insights

Cross-Reference Version (CRV)

3. Say it

4. Pray it

7:5-6

Prayer to Jesus

Thanksgiving

Commitment

Jesus' Response

Creative Worship

Song 7:7-9

⁷ This thy stature is like to a palm tree, and thy breasts to clusters of grapes. ⁸ I said, I will go up to the palm tree, I will take hold of the boughs thereof: now also thy breasts shall be as clusters of the vine, and the smell of thy nose like apples; ⁹ And the roof of thy mouth like the best wine for my beloved, that goeth down sweetly, causing the lips of those that are asleep to speak.

date

1. Read it

2. Write it

Alternate Bible Version

Personal Paraphrase Version (PPV)

Key Words

Questions

Insights

Cross-Reference Version (KJV)

3. Say it

4. Pray it

7:7-9

Prayer to Jesus

Thanksgiving

Commitment

Jesus' Response

Creative Worship

Song 7:10

[10] I am my beloved's,
and his desire is
toward me.

date

1. Read it

2. Write it

Alternate Bible Version

Personal Paraphrase Version (PPV)

Key Words

Questions

Insights

Cross-Reference Version (KJV)

3. Say it

4. Pray it

7:10

Prayer to Jesus

Thanksgiving

Commitment

Jesus' Response

Creative Worship

Song 7:11-12

¹¹ Come, my beloved, let us go forth into the field; let us lodge in the villages. ¹² Let us get up early to the vineyards; let us see if the vine flourish, whether the tender grape appear, and the pomegranates bud forth: there will I give thee my loves.

date

1. Read it

2. Write it

Alternate Bible Version

Personal Paraphrase Version (PPV)

Key Words

Questions

Insights

Cross-Reference Version (CRV)

3. Say it

7:11-12

4. Pray it

Prayer to Jesus

Thanksgiving

Commitment

Jesus' Response

Creative Worship

Song 7:13

¹³ The mandrakes give a smell, and at our gates are all manner of pleasant fruits, new and old, which I have laid up for thee, O my beloved.

date

1. Read it

2. Write it

Alternate Bible Version

Personal Paraphrase Version (PPV)

Key Words

Questions

Insights

Cross-Reference Version (KJV)

3. Say it

4. Pray it

7:13

Prayer to Jesus

_____

_____

_____

_____

Thanksgiving

_____

_____

_____

_____

Commitment

_____

_____

_____

_____

Jesus' Response

_____

_____

_____

_____

Creative Worship

Song of Solomon | 8

¹ O that thou wert as my brother, that sucked the breasts of my mother! when I should find thee without, I would kiss thee; yea, I should not be despised. ² I would lead thee, and bring thee into my mother's house, who would instruct me: I would cause thee to drink of spiced wine of the juice of my pomegranate. ³ His left hand should be under my head, and his right hand should embrace me. ⁴ I charge you, O daughters of Jerusalem, that ye stir not up, nor awake my love, until he please. ⁵ Who is this that cometh up from the wilderness, leaning upon her beloved? I raised thee up under the apple tree: there thy mother brought thee forth: there she brought thee forth that bare thee. ⁶ Set me as a seal upon thine heart, as a seal upon thine arm: for love is strong as death; jealousy is cruel as the grave: the coals thereof are coals of fire, which hath a most vehement flame. ⁷ Many waters cannot quench love, neither can the floods drown it: if a man would give all the substance of his house for love, it would utterly be contemned. ⁸ We have a little sister, and she hath no breasts: what shall we do for our sister in the day when she shall be spoken for? ⁹ If she be a wall, we will build upon her a palace of silver: and if she be a door, we will inclose her with boards of cedar. ¹⁰ I am a wall, and my breasts like towers: then was I in his eyes as one that found favour. ¹¹ Solomon had a vineyard at Baalhamon; he let out the vineyard unto keepers; every one for the fruit thereof was to bring a thousand pieces of silver. ¹² My vineyard, which is mine, is before me: thou, O Solomon, must have a thousand, and those that keep the fruit thereof two hundred. ¹³ Thou that dwellest in the gardens, the companions hearken to thy voice: cause me to hear it. ¹⁴ Make haste, my beloved, and be thou like to a roe or to a young hart upon the mountains of spices.

Chapter Eight Overview

Our journey into Bridal Partnership with Jesus is eventually expressed through humility and boldness in public ministry as well as full union and communion with the Lord.

We long to boldly display our affections for Jesus but recognize the need to walk with humility and restraint. We prayerfully discern how to express our intimatcy with Jesus publicly in ways that will edify others (1 Cor. 14:12). The Lord allows us to bring His presence into the most difficult places so that the name of Jesus may be exalted. In trying circumstances God's invisible work supports us. His loving intervention leads us through this strategic season.

The Holy Spirit prepares us to emerge from the wilderness with loving and leaning hearts, the ultimate purpose of this journey. If we surrender our lives to Jesus and follow Him through every season we come forth as His victorious Bride. God uses weakness to manifest His power and strength (2 Cor. 12:9). He is our Divine source and great reward.

The eighth revelation of Jesus in the Song is the **Consuming Fire**. This is the most well known passage from the Song of Solomon. In the great climax, Jesus reminds us of how He awakened our hearts and invites us to receive His Bridal seal of Divine love.

We each commence our journey with His kiss and conclude it with His seal of love. The fire of God's passionate zeal for us forever empowers our hearts with supernatural love. This eternal flame of love will withstand the rivers of persecution and floods of temptation. Jesus Christ's love for us has conquered the grave. No opposition can prevent Him from bringing us into full maturity if we walk in obedience to our Beloved!

Our spiritual identity now flows from God's evaluation of our beauty. This assurance gives us confidence to walk in partnership with the Lord. We are aware of our accountability to tend our own vineyards (hearts) and lead others into fruitfulness. With urgency we intercede for the Church to be brought into full maturity and for Jesus' return (Rev. 22:17, 20).

Song 8:1-3

1. Read it

¹ O that thou wert as my brother, that sucked the breasts of my mother! when I should find thee without, I would kiss thee; yea, I should not be despised. ² I would lead thee, and bring thee into my mother's house, who would instruct me: I would cause thee to drink of spiced wine of the juice of my pomegranate. ³ His left hand should be under my head, and his right hand should embrace me.

2. Write it

Alternate Bible Version

_____

_____

_____

_____

_____

Personal Paraphrase Version (PPV)

_____

_____

_____

_____

_____

_____

_____

Key Words

Questions

Insights

Cross-Reference Version (KJV)

3. Say it

4. Pray it

8:1-3

Prayer to Jesus

Thanksgiving

Commitment

Jesus' Response

Creative Worship

Song 8:4

⁴ I charge you, O daughters of Jerusalem,
that ye stir not up, nor awake my love,
until he please.

date

1. Read it

2. Write it

Alternate Bible Version

Personal Paraphrase Version (PPV)

Key Words

Questions

Insights

Cross-Reference Version (CRV)

3. Say it

4. Pray it

8:4

Prayer to Jesus

Thanksgiving

Commitment

Jesus' Response

Creative Worship

Song 8:5

date

1. Read it

2. Write it

⁵ Who is this that cometh up
from the wilderness,
leaning upon her beloved?
I raised thee up under
the apple tree: there thy
mother brought thee forth:
there she brought thee
forth that bare thee.

Alternate Bible Version

Personal Paraphrase Version (PPV)

Key Words

Questions

Insights

Cross-Reference Version (CRV)

3. Say it

4. Pray it

8:5

Prayer to Jesus

Thanksgiving

Commitment

Jesus' Response

Creative Worship

Song 8:6-7

⁶ Set me as a seal upon thine heart, as a seal upon thine arm: for love is strong as death; jealousy is cruel as the grave: the coals thereof are coals of fire, which hath a most vehement flame. ⁷ Many waters cannot quench love, neither can the floods drown it: if a man would give all the substance of his house for love, it would utterly be contemned.

date

1. Read it

2. Write it

Alternate Bible Version

Personal Paraphrase Version (PPV)

Key Words

Questions

Insights

Cross-Reference Version (KJV)

3. Say it

4. Pray it

8:6-7

Prayer to Jesus

Thanksgiving

Commitment

Jesus' Response

Creative Worship

Song 8:8-10

8 We have a little sister, and she hath no breasts: what shall we do for our sister in the day when she shall be spoken for? 9 If she be a wall, we will build upon her a palace of silver: and if she be a door, we will inclose her with boards of cedar. 10 I am a wall, and my breasts like towers: then was I in his eyes as one that found favour.

date

1. Read it

2. Write it

Alternate Bible Version

Personal Paraphrase Version (PPV)

Key Words

Questions

Insights

Cross-Reference Version (CRV)

3. Say it

4. Pray it

8:8-10

Prayer to Jesus

Thanksgiving

Commitment

Jesus' Response

Creative Worship

Song 8:11-12

¹¹ Solomon had a vineyard at Baalhamon; he let out the vineyard unto keepers; every one for the fruit thereof was to bring a thousand pieces of silver. ¹² My vineyard, which is mine, is before me: thou, O Solomon, must have a thousand, and those that keep the fruit thereof two hundred.

date

1. Read it

2. Write it

Alternate Bible Version

Personal Paraphrase Version

Key Words

Questions

Insights

Cross-Reference Version (CRV)

3. Say it

4. Pray it

8:11-12

Prayer to Jesus

Thanksgiving

Commitment

Jesus' Response

Creative Worship

Song 8:13–14

date

1. Read it

2. Write it

¹³ Thou that dwellest in the gardens,
the companions hearken to
thy voice: cause me to hear it.
¹⁴ Make haste, my beloved,
and be thou like to a roe
or to a young hart
upon the mountains
of spices.

Alternate Bible Version

Personal Paraphrase Version (PPV)

Key Words

Questions

Insights

Cross-Reference Version (KJV)

3. Say it

4. Pray it

8:13-14

Prayer to Jesus

Thanksgiving

Commitment

Jesus' Response

Creative Worship

My *life* is the poem that *God* has writ,

so I will both live and

utter it!

Chérie Blair
Revised from quote by
Henry David Thoreau

The End

or just the beginning...

Our journey through the Romance of the Gospel has only just begun. We could study the Song of Solomon for the rest of our lives and only barely scratch the surface of everything that God would communicate to us of His affections and our role as His Divine partner for eternity.

The intent of this study tool is to provoke us. Will we make this Divine Love Song our lifelong pursuit as we continue this journey into the Romance of the Gospel and Bridal partnership with the King of the ages?

We may read and comprehend the direction this journey is leading us, but in reality we are still back at the initial longing for the Divine Kiss of God's Word upon our hearts. At times, we may experience various stages of the journey simultaneously or find that we are in the same season for several years. Whether or not we have studied the Song of Solomon before, we can relate it to different periods of our lives. The Song simply provides a road map to guide us along our journey. Turning this romantic poetry into devotional prayer helps solidify the foundation of love in our hearts so that we will not be shaken in the midst of adversity.

When I discovered Jesus as my eternal Bridegroom through the Song I began to write, sing, paint, and dance with Divine creativity. My identity shifted from what I 'do' to who I 'am' before the Lord. Jesus reminds me daily that I ravish His heart with one glance. A single movement of my heart toward my Beloved overwhelms His heart with love for me. And yet, I have only begun to understand what it means to partner with Him as a flowing brook of abundant blessing that carries His refreshing love into the valley of this world. I am just now learning to pray that the Body of Christ would come forth in maturity though I myself have so far to go before entering into the fullness of love and union with My Beloved, Jesus Christ. May we continue on this journey together until one day we stand before our Lord as His pure and spotless Bride!

My *soul* shall be *satisfied...*

Psalm 63:5

Closing Word
by Audra D. Close

As I reflect over the past six years I am amazed at the godly transformation that I have witnessed in Cherie's life. I know that this is due in large part to the revelation that she received in 2002 of Jesus as her Eternal Bridegroom. I also credit her accelerated spiritual growth to the amount of time that she has invested reading, writing, praying, dancing, painting and singing the Word of God, especially the Song of all Songs. Our relationship with Jesus is truly not about how much we do or how perfect we think we have done the job. Our Love Walk with the Lord is about being enjoyed by the most passionate, merciful, loving being in the universe — the Creator of all — and enjoying Him without fear or shame. Truth brings freedom. As we continue down this little path of exploring the Scriptures we will be released into greater levels of love, fulfillment, and joy with our Bridegroom King as well as with our brothers and sisters in Christ.

We are all so BUSY in today's world, a frantic pace being the norm for most of us, in order to 'get it all done.' I encourage you — no, I admonish you as well as myself — to continue the journey of discovering the treasures and mysteries of God. Let us not give up; no matter what the circumstances we must continue gathering oil as did the wise virgins in Matthew 25:1-13. If we do not actually make the time to gather oil, to spend time in the secret place with Jesus, we will wake up one day to find out that we have run out of time. However, if we eat our daily bread (Deut. 8:3; Matt. 4:4; 6:11), spending time in the Word with the Word of Life, our investments will yield eternal dividends. For the time is drawing near and the night is short. Soon we shall hear the voice of the Bridegroom thundering in response to the Spirit and the Bride who are crying, "Come, Lord Jesus, come" (Rev. 22:17, 20)!

Audra D. Close, Staff
International House of Prayer of Kansas City

*W*hy so cold, Oh heart of mine?
    Why refuse such love Divine?

Come, Oh Lord, and tenderize ~
    This hardened heart that's bought the lies,
"He loves you not; you're filthy and poor ~
    You can't even earn it; just look at your score!"

But You tell me how I've stolen your heart ~
    When all I have done is a dance and some art.
    I'm not even worthy;
    Can't You see that I'm dirty?

    Don't stare at me; I'm dark.
        You'll see a bruise, a scar, a mark ~
    Where I once let love in,
        But was wounded by men.

    Yet, I long to know this love ~
        Of One who calls me His dove.
    Why should I hide behind a veil?
        Must I remain locked in this cell?

Come quickly, my Lover; do not delay ~
    Kiss me with Your Word, and take me away.
Your love to me is more delightful than wine ~
    Oh, satisfy my heart with the fruits of Your Vine!

by Chérie Blair ~ Uniquedove Creations © 2007
(Song 1:2,4,6-7; 4:9,12; 6:9)

...*there is none* upon earth that *I desire* besides You.

My flesh and my heart fail; *But God* is the strength of my heart, and my portion *forever.*

Psalm 73:25-26 NKJV

*D*o not stare at me because I am dark.

I know the depravity of my sin ~
The deceitfulness of my heart within.

Declare the loveliness God sees in me ~
That a 'lover' may become my identity.

Speak the truth that will set me free ~
Transforming these ashes into beauty.

Do not stare at me because I am dark.

View me through the blood of Christ ~
The window 'pain' of His sacrifice.

For though my sins are red; I know ~
They will be washed white as snow!

It's true I am wretched, naked, and poor,
Yet through me God displays His splendor.

Do not stare at me because I am dark.

Envision me before the King of all kings ~
A pure, spotless Bride ~ a fragrant offering.

For though I am dark; I am lovely!

He will purify me with the fire of His love ~
That I may become His perfect Uniquedove.

by Chérie Blair ~ Uniquedove Creations © 2007
(Song 1:5-6; 6:9; 8:6; Is. 61:3; Jer. 17:9; 2 Cor. 11:2; Rev 3:17)

With just One Glance...

You Ravish My heart!

Song 4:9 CBPV

To purchase devotionals, artwork, or
make a donation, please visit:

www.uniquedove.com

Visit the International House of Prayer and
join us for LIVE 24/7 worship on the internet at:

www.ihop.org

Biographies

visit us online!

Chérie Blair
Uniquedove Creations
www.uniquedove.com

Chérie has been involved in ministry at the
International House of Prayer (IHOP) Missions
Base in Kansas City, Missouri, since 2003.
During times of worship she expresses the testimony of Jesus through
music, dance, and art. Many of Chérie's artistic designs give visual
expression to Scriptural truth intended to lead you into deeper study
of God's Word. Each unique 'creation' is a gift from her Beloved, Jesus.
Her prayer is that you may experience the everlasting love of Jesus
Christ and be filled with the Spirit of God (Eph. 3:19).

Mike Bickle
International House of Prayer
www.ihop.org

Mike is the Director of the International House
of Prayer and President of the Forerunner
School of Ministry in Kansas City, Missouri.
He has authored several books including Passion for Jesus, Growing
in the Prophetic, The Pleasures of Loving God, After God's Own Heart,
The Rewards of Fasting: Experiencing the Emotions and Power of God,
and The Seven Longings of the Human Heart. His teaching emphasizes
how to grow in passion for Jesus through intimacy with God.

To purchase CDs, books, and other materials
on the Song of Solomon, please visit:

www.ihop.org/shop

for your journey

Song of Songs CD Series (includes notes)
Mike Bickle

The Song of Songs is Mike Bickle's most popular
teaching series. Mike has devoted over ten years
of prayerful study and research covering each line of this Divine Love Song.
This is Mike's completely revised and updated course on Songs of Songs
— his most comprehensive and powerful presentation of this glorious book
to date. This 20-CD set contains the study guide in PDF format. This series
will help you make sense of your own journey.

The Seven Longings of the Human Heart
Mike Bickle

God has placed deep longings in the heart of every human being.
We all long for beauty, for greatness, for fascination, for intimacy. We all long
to be enjoyed, to be whole-hearted, to make a lasting impact.

Many of us have been taught to deny these longings. We've been told they
are not of God. But the problem is not the longings — they are given of God
and cannot be denied. Problems only arise when we attempt to fulfill godly,
legitimate longings in ungodly, wrong ways.

Only God can fulfill the longings He has given to us. Only God can truly satisfy
the deepest longings of our hearts. When we realize our longings are godly
and God wants to fulfill them, we find freedom and joy. We experience intimacy
with God in ways we would have never thought possible.

Printed in the United States
206006BV00001B/63/A

9 780615 173740